Lightning
and
Honey

CW00336359

Books by Xian

Raven

Lightning and Honey

Lightning

and

Honey

XIAN

PALMETTO
PUBLISHING

Charleston, SC
www.PalmettoPublishing.com

Illustrations by Brianna Tischler

Copyright © 2024 by Xian

All All rights reserved. This book or any portion thereof may not be re-
produced or used in any manner whatsoever without the express written
permission of the publisher except for the use of brief quotations in a
book review.

Paperback: 979-8-8229-4137-3

Contents

About Lightning and Honey

Lightning and Honey endures drug abuse, starting a new journey, depression, anxiety, finding your worth within, finding the one you love, divorce, physical abuse, heartbreak, death, celebration, finding your own light, growth, life, being alone, rising and falling, lies, leaving, love, taking, and giving. *Lightning and Honey* is about dealing with family or someone you know who is a drug addict, starting new journeys, kicking depression and anxiety in the balls, and so much more.

Note from the Author

This book is not for anyone under the age of sixteen.
I wrote *Lightning and Honey* in hopes that this book will help my readers understand the different types of struggles people go through in their daily lives. This book does not pertain to everyone, or anyone in particular. *Lightning and Honey* is for a mature audience only.

Thank you, lovely readers.
Love,
Xian

Trigger Warnings

- Drug abuse
- Depression
- Anxiety
- Divorce
- Physical abuse
- Heartbreak
- Death
- Being alone
- Lies

Heroin

Does it hurt?
"Sometimes."
What do you do to stop the pain?
"I close my eyes."

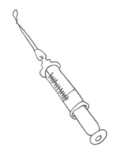

Pride

The honey drips from her mouth,
sweet like elderberry.
Purple stains on her lips,
she marches toward me.
"Don't worry baby, this is the beginning of us."
These soft words are what poured out of
her mouth before she became my wife.

Mask

Don't be fooled by the men with jigsaw
faces, they bleed too.

Perfect Timing

Don't lose your mind.
Simply take a deep breath.
Don't go searching for acceptance.
You were born to stand out.
Don't chase a dream
if you didn't wake up to make it a reality.

Depression

I can't do this anymore.
The stress is gnawing in my stomach.
I don't want to drown in my own tears.
Anxiety gives me a friendly reminder that
they will always be here when it's unexpected.
The muscles in my tongue have weakened.
"When will this get better?"
A question I never had the answer to.
I demanded the hire ups to give me hope,
for my only fear is hanging from the ceiling.
"In due time child, in due time."

Note to Self

Dear future me,
We live in a world where people
will try to break you down.
You mustn't let them.
Dear future me,
We live in a world that is cold.
Please bundle up.
Dear future me,
We live in a world that is bitter.
Level out your tastebuds,
and remember everything isn't sweet.
Dear future me,
Overall, no matter how many times
this world breaks you down,
feeds you sour lies,
or gives you frostbite,
just remember
you are you no matter what.

This Marriage is Sweet

Lemons and limes,
strawberries and blueberries,
watermelons and honey
are what I shove in my mouth
the morning of my wedding day.

Growth Takes Time

I'm tired of being a dandelion
in a field full of sunflowers.
I'm tired of being a caterpillar
in a cage full of butterflies.
I'm tired of being an egg
living in a hive with worker bees.
But my time will come when I can sprout
my wings and leave a petal everywhere I go.

Unreal

We have met in my mind more times
than I can remember,
daydreaming about the day I would
get to smell the scent of your hair.
We have met in my dreams several times.
You have spoken to my soul with
sweet lullaby words,
injecting my brain with intelligence not found
in textbooks.
It's sad this is just a dream.

A Divorced Snake

Men say women have mind control.
Men say women speak poison from their lips.
They slither like snakes into a married man's bed.
But nobody else talks about what the man does.

Spoken Mind

I want someone who invites my intelligence in,
someone who doesn't run from it.

When Envy Takes Control

I envy the rain for pouring down your body
where my hands used to be.
I envy your pillow at night.
It's greedy with the scent of your hair fresh out
of the shower.
I envy the sunshine, blazing across
your face that my lips once rested on.
Most of all, I envy your feelings for leaving me.

Finding the Light

Heartbreak is one thing,
soul-breaking is another.

Marriage Without Divorce

A swimming pool filled with
tears of mothers who have lost
unborn souls,
half-empty beer cans spilled on the sofa
from an unemployed father.
A marriage ring that sits on the nightstand
collecting dust no longer holds
a purpose.

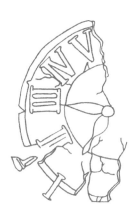

Dead Petals

The moon becomes sun,
sun becomes moon.
As the day changes,
so does my breath,
getting thinner and thinner
until my lungs have dried up
like the roses you gave me on our
anniversary of five years.
Carnations, were they?

A Dying Widow

I can taste her on your lips.
The stain from her lipstick is
infused to the fibers on your
white work shirt.
I'm guessing cherry red is the color.
The scent of her perfume
weakens my stomach,
knots my heart,
takes every hope I had
of our future and turns it into mud,
blood boiling like shower water
you washed with to scrub her touch off your body
but can never get clean enough to
lay in bed next to me.
Early morning, you're gone.
You say it's "business"
but you are just putting your business in her.
You say it's nothing.
Men have needs.
What about my needs?
Exactly nine months pass, and you have a child,
not born from my organs

but from hers.
Struggling to put this past me
like I did with our first unborn child,
I have no reason to stay.
I have no belief in saving our marriage.
But still, I stay.
I am lost without you.
I am lost without the person
who shattered my heart into a
million tiny pieces.
I am lost without the person who
sold me tornado lies.
I lost myself to the person who
crushed me one thousand times
and without a doubt will do it again.
That person is my husband.

Light

I do not wish to have you
to fill the empty parts of me.
I want to be full on my own.
I do not crave your words of wisdom.
I want to develop my own dictionary.
I do not care for your unwanted
opinions that drip out of your mouth
like a broken faucet.
I hold my own light, and if you dare to look
too close, it might just burn your eyes.

Cheers to All the Women Surviving Abuse

Cheers to me for cementing my broken
pieces back together.
Cheers to me for holding back tears I once
shed for an unwanted soul.
Cheers to me for getting out, barely alive.

I Am

I am not broken because of the depression.
I am not invisible because of the anxiety.
I am not small because of the tasteful rumors
spilled about me.
I am whole.
I am complete.
I am a person.

Till Death Do Us Part

You sold my soul for half the price it's worth.
You told my mother you would take care of me
when I was sick, but here you are, selling my
organs for half the price of what they're worth.
You played games with my youngest brother,
promising him you will always be around, but here
you are, selling my heart for a dime.
You told my father you would take my hand in
marriage
till death do us part, but here you are, selling my
ring finger with the ring still attached.
Seven years with who I thought was the love of
my life ended up being a horror story
I knew I wouldn't survive.
So take my pieces.
Take my body parts.
Rip them limb from limb.
Sell them for whatever price you want.
But truth be told, nobody is going to want
pieces of a broken-down wife.
You don't even want them.

Optimism

There's a light at the end of my tunnel.
It's not very bright, but it's there.

Growing Up

Honeybees.
Wildflowers.
Rainbows.
Sunshine.
Four main characters of my story
that I need to survive adulthood.

New Beginnings

Eyes locked,
arms twisted,
bodies pressed.
Holding her used to be a dream,
and now it's a reality.

Embrace Life

Allow yourself to be foolish when falling in love.
Allow yourself to make mistakes; it's a part of
growing up.
Allow yourself to spin outside, embracing the
summer air.
Allow yourself to feel happy, but just remember:
Everything isn't peaches and cream.

Imperfectly Perfected

The perfect person doesn't exist,
not in real life at least.

Not Alone

What a relief it is to discover
that I'm not the only
person with a broken soul.
I am not the only person with
a broken heart.
I am not the only person that is broken.

Different Forms Of Anxiety

Dangling off the side of a bridge,
fingertips cramping,
having no fear of falling.
Is this what anxiety feels like?

Blindness

You take the blade,
press it against your wrists,
numb to the pain,
unaware of what lies in the afterlife.

Patients is a Virtue

You do not just wake up
and become the butterfly
you wish to see if you do
not take the proper steps
to grow your wings.

Your Future Wife

I am not perfect.
My teeth aren't straight.
My hair is a matted mess.
I have freckles and moles.
My legs are short.
I grow hair under my armpits.
I have hair on my arms.
My eyebrows aren't even.
I am clumsy.
Do you still love me?

Don't Waste Your Time

Searching for happiness,
with all the time wasted, I grew old.
The happiness was waiting for me
and grew impatient.
I died without my happiness.

Not a Voicemail

The front end will talk shit to you
just like you talk shit to my back end.
The only difference is my front end
isn't scared to dish out your words of
terror, and my back end doesn't give a fuck.

Not Different

We all feel loneliness sometimes.
Don't think you're different just because
you hide yours.

Find Yourself Not in Others

The beating of your heartbeat
takes my breath away. It
lets me know you're still living.
But who are you truly living for?
Because it's not for yourself.

Filling Your Life with Mines

It's okay for a honeybee to suck the
life out of the tulips that grow in your
yard, but it's not okay for you to suck
the life out of my lilies.
Learn when to stop.

Love is a Gift

I promised myself
the last one was the one.
Now here I am again, redefining
"the one,"
wishing the "last" one was real.

Personal Footprint

Don't compare your path to others.
Everyone is on a different trail.
Follow your own.

New Flower

To survive you need to be able to
fall,
wilt,
rise,
root.
Only then will you bloom.

Home is Where the Heart is

When lightning booms, you take shelter
in my arms.
When the snow falls, we sleep together
like two rabbits hibernating.
When the sky cries tears,
my heart is where you will take
shelter and stay dry.

The Hate You Give

Sensitive to the words you speak,
crying at the hate you give.
Why must you shut me out
when I am at my lowest?
Don't flag me away when you
see the disgust on my face.
Don't turn your back on me.
If you say you love me,
we can make this work.
Don't leave me locked in a
closet alone to die.

Leaving the Nest

My story isn't nice.
I bleed.
I cry.
I break down.
But after all of that, I bloom.
I sprout.
I found my wings.
Now it's time to fly.

Sharing Your Happiness is Not a Crime

Happiness—
a feeling I thought I'd never have,
an idea I thought only existed to some
but now is a feeling I love,
a feeling that I'm never giving up on,
a feeling I wish to give to others.

Burn it All Down

You light a match it my heart,
watching it spread like wildfire.
You made me believe that
being silent is what keeps me alive.
You have changed my world completely,
telling me repeatedly,
"You are nothing without me."
And I let you. I let you speak down
to me, manipulate me, torture me.
But in that spare moment,
your actions no longer hurt me.
Your words no longer break me down.
Your true nature will spill out like a wildfire and
burn everything you love to the ground.

Simple Life

Honeybees reflect the sun,
buzzing around, bringing nature everywhere they
go,
sucking on elderberries and wildflowers.
I wish to be a honeybee.

A Day Without Clouds

Lightning doesn't thunder twice.
Let that be a lesson.
Loving doesn't only come once
in a lifetime.
Choose wisely.

Distress

Why do you hurt yourself?
"It helps take the pain away."
But you're hurting others too.

Rise

We all watch the same sunset.
It might be at different times,
and at different parts of the world,
but it's still the same sunset.

Uncontrollable

"This is a man's world!"
is what people would scream at me when
I walked out of the house
not dressed in the most modest clothes.
"My body my choice!"
is what I would scream back.

Brave

What is the greatest lesson women should learn?
You have everything you need.
Don't let the world tell you different.

Baby Boy

My body is not your battleground,
nor is my body your playground.
I have no children to raise,
so don't think I am going to sit
here and raise you while
you suck on my titty, asking for more.

A War Between Two Lovers

What we build will break me,
and I know it.
But still, we stay and fight until the end.

I Don't Need a Museum

Your art isn't supposed to be liked
by every person in the world.
If your heart likes your work,
if your soul likes your work,
then why does it matter what other people think?

Envy

How am I supposed to shake this envy I hold in my
heart?
How am I supposed to just get up and walk away
when
I gave you my soul?
This envy is eating me alive.
I can feel it rotting in my bones.
There's not a day that goes by that I wish you would
feel
this envy just like I do.
There's not a day that goes by that I don't think
about
how empty I am.
My love, my life, my heart, and my soul—
come take this envy away.
I do not wish to pass this on to my future husband.

The Birthplace of All Humanity

Don't hide your blood and milk.
The womb and breast fed everyone.

Climbing Mountains

Slow down and enjoy the view.
You worked so hard to be here.

Temple

There is no home like your body.
There is no safety like your body.
There is no shelter like your body.
There is no…you get the picture.

Camouflage

When the world gives you pain,
don't cry.
Make gold out of it.

Queen

Wear your crown high,
tighten it on your head,
don't let it fall,
wear it proudly.

Kind Soul

How is it so easy for you to be kind to people
when people have not been so kind to you?
"Ugly does not live in my soul."

The Summer Slumber

Here on firefly lane, honeybees lay their heads to
rest.
Flowers bring in their petals for the night.
The summer air begins to set in and the
stars are glowing like fireflies.

My Personal Pot of Coffee

Love streams in like a
fresh cup of hot coffee.
Laughs are the stream of my consciousness.
Dedication is what drives me.
Stability keeps me aroused in ways
I can't express with words.

We No Longer Sell Doormats

I'm too in love with
my life to lay on the floor, waiting
for the next man
to walk all over me like a doormat.

Self-love should be endured by everyone
and taught by everyone.

Paradise

Take a journey with me into
my soul.
There you will find
sour milk
and rotting lilies.
But most of all,
you will find me lost
in the sea of lovers who have
let me go a thousand times.

This is My Place

Broken bones heal.
Tears dry up.
And you can wash the
stained blood from your shirt,
but I am permanent.

Music to My Ears

Lightning adds color to the sky.
Rain waters the earth, soothing
all forms of drought.
Thunder creates music.
Some can't bear to hear it boom.

Mother's Love

The facts are,
nobody is going to
love you as much as your mother.

You're in the Wrong Crowd

Stop trying to prove yourself
to a crowd that doesn't know
you exist.

Don't Be Weak

When I strip you of your
humanity like you did
mine,
don't cry.
Toughen up.

Stuck in the Afterlife

Fire.
Flesh.
Blood.
Flames.
You call this life?
I call it hell.

Someone Call the Trash Man

The wisdom of "wise" men set in my
skin like an underlying rash.
The words of "grown" men follow
me around like a rotten stench.
You say I need you; my life would
be empty without you.
Truth be told, I take out the trash daily,
so what makes you think I need your trash
juice rotting in my soul?

Boogeyman

Severe burns to my limbs.
Severed heartaches.
Lose ties and strange lies.
You build me up to break me down.
Cement and concrete can no
longer hold me together.
Your fingers have become one with
a sledgehammer, and I have become
one with gorilla glue. But even that's
not strong enough to hold together
the broken pieces that fall off when I
roll out of bed in the morning.
You claim you love me,
and I want to believe you.
You say you're going to take care
of me as you clean the bloody masterpiece
off my face you created with your fist.
People have warned me about the
boogeyman that stands stiff in the
deep end of your closet and waits for
you to fall fast asleep before he attacks.
You are my boogeyman, and I am your victim.
I don't know how to wake up from this dream,
so this is where I will place my tombstone
and lay to rest while my boogeyman finds
a new victim to suck into his soul.

Sorry, Wrong Person

Am I broken? Yes.
Is my heart sore? Yes.
Am I going to keep taking it as
you push up against me?
No!
Go find someone else who is
willing to lay there silently as
you abuse their body.

From Mother to Child

My mother used to rock
me to bed every night.
The feeling of her hand on
my back became more soothing
with every stroke. As I got older,
she stopped rocking me, only because
I am twenty-four now and too big to
fit in her lap, but I occasionally rock
myself when I want her to soothe me to sleep.

Packed Bags and Gone With the Wind

The stream of tears that run off your face
creates a soaked tsunami on your shirt.
The pain and agony is a painted mask that
fits too snug on your emotionless face.
You reach your arms out for me in hopes
I wouldn't walk out of the door.
You're screaming and begging me to stay,
but under all that fake frustration, I can hear the truth,
and your truth is rottener than expired eggs.
That's exactly what happened here:
Our marriage is more expired than rotten eggs,
and I'm tired of filtering out the drain hole
that holds more lies than I can remember.
So no, I will not stay. I will not clean your
snot-nosed, tear-filled face. That's your own
problem.

Pulling Away Without Hurting You

She's holding my hand, and I can feel her
heartbeat through her veins, specifically her
ring finger, on which I have placed a rock.
She looks at me with such happiness and joy.
How do I tell her that when I look at her,
I don't see the same thing? She is not the person
I fell in love with. She's changed for
the worse, and I'm not sure
I can fasten my seatbelt for this ride.
How do I tell my wife of six years that our
relationship has run its course? She is no longer
the one for me. She is not the person I love
anymore.

Endless Love

My love for you is like the ocean.
My waves come crashing down on you,
and no matter how small your boat is, you
always manage to make your way back to
shore and set sail again.

Bean

Never have I imagined sitting here with you.
Watching you brush your hair that you crave
to get chopped or simply watching you get
dressed brings me to a different happy place
that I only experience when I'm with you.
Thank you for feeding my soul.

Therapy

Lightning strikes me down.
Laying on the hard concrete,
I can smell the rain coming.
The first raindrop hits my chest,
then a sea of drops takes over the city.
The smell of fresh rain is like honey in my
cup of tea. There's nothing more
relaxing than the sound of pouring rain
and being drenched in it.

Prayers

You're praying for time,
I'm praying for sanity.
You're praying for safety,
I'm praying for strength.
We are praying for different things,
but we are still human.

Let Me Fight My Battles

Why are you breathing heavy?
You would have thought that this
was your struggle and not mine.
Sit down, relax. I got this.

Chambers of Hearts

Follow me darling. Let me lead you to a world
of paradise that hides in my heart. Just promise
me one thing: When you see the great world of
wonders, don't destroy it, for it will suck
you in and dry you bloodless.
Do you dare to come in and take a peek?

Drowning in My Sorrows

I'm a madman.
I threw myself into the sea,
sinking to the bottom of the ocean.
No one ever mentions the beautiful
lights the water holds.
I am not mad at myself.
Let me enjoy this view on my way
down to my death.
The crystal water submerges me.
My father would be disappointed in me,
but the sea is where I came from, and
the sea is where I belong,
so the sea is where I will return to,
satisfied with my underwater family,
never to be seen again by human eyes.

In Pairs We Go

Fill me with your lies.
Take my blood.
Don't be afraid of the afterlife,
because you're coming with me when I die.

This is What We Call War

I told you the truth.
I begged for you to believe me.
I know her lipstick stains and
spilled perfume in the bed say different,
but I promise you, baby, I'm telling
you the truth.

Sell Me Price Tags I Cannot Afford

Diamonds.
Pearls.
Silver
and gold.
All just objects.
No meaning behind it.

Killing Children

Hush now child,
rest your head.
Dream of soft silk butterflies.
When you wake up, the bad men
will have disappeared.

Level

I am not a warrior,
I am not a killer.
However, do push me to
my limit and you will
see what lays behind this
pretty little mask.

ER

My fingers are numb.
My eyes are burning.
My brain is disconnected.
My soul has left.
Is this what death feels like?

My Little Honeybee

Honeybee wings
like stained glass.
So fragile,
transparent.
So beautiful to look at.
Take these details and carry
them on with you into your next life.
Wear your stained-glass honeybee
wings with pride. Remember your true colors.

Accountability

People's reaction to
you holding them
accountable is not your
burden to carry or your
worry to have, and it never will be.

Power Abuse

You burn me with your words,
smack me with your smart remarks.
"You will be nothing without me."
He carved those words into my arm so many times,
I started to believe it.

Gone

Standing in a room with all my loved ones,
am I the only one who can see them?

Bad Man

I can smell your intentions
from a mile away,
your smug smile,
evil grin,
and your boner
that you get when you see
a female passing by.

About the Author

Growing up with a life filled with words and a movie projector in my brain, it was only natural that I, Xian, start writing my own books. I'm constantly finding new things to write about, but first, as always, the words form a motion picture in my brain before they become permanent on paper. Music and good scenery are my top two things that help me write. The inspiration that helped me write *Lightning and Honey* is the fact that everyone goes through different struggles every day—doesn't matter what it is or what it looks like. Some people wear their struggles on their face, and others hide it. I wrote *Lightning and Honey* in hopes of having my readers understand that not every day is peaches and cream for everyone. So remember, when someone asks for help, help them any way you can. When someone needs a hug, hold them tight. When someone needs a shoulder to cry on, grab a box of tissues and let that person cry. Yes, your shirt is going to be filled with tears and snot, but you can wash it.

Milton Keynes UK
Ingram Content Group UK Ltd.
UKHW010853280324
440101UK00001B/241